Jewish Values in Genesis: If I Could Ask Abraham

Lesson Plan Manual

By Rachael Gelfman Schultz

Behrman House, Inc.
www.behrmanhouse.com/values-bible

Library of Congress Cataloging-in-Publication Data

Schultz, Rachael Gelfman, author.

Jewish values in Genesis : if I could ask Abraham : lesson plan manual / by Rachael Gelfman Schultz.

pages cm

"This work consists of two complementary books. The Student Response Journal includes creative, interactive activities, integrating Jewish texts with journal writing, drama, art, music, movement, and more. The Teacher Resource presents 14 ready-to-use lesson plans of approximately 50 minutes each for Jewish Values in Genesis: If I Could Ask Abraham. It includes suggestions for teaching every element of the Student Response Journal."--Introduction.

ISBN 978-0-87441-926-9

1. Bible. Genesis--Study and teaching (Elementary). 2. Jewish ethics--Study and teaching (Elementary) 3. Jewish religious education--Teaching methods. I. Title.

BS1239.S382 2015

296.6'8083--dc23

2014046364

Design: AURAS Design

Springfield, New Jersey 07081
www.behrmanhouse.com

ISBN 978-0-87441-926-9
Printed in the United States of America

Visit www.behrmanhouse.com/values-bible for more resources.

Contents

Introduction

How can the Torah help us to become our best selves and build healthy family relationships? *Jewish Values in Genesis: If I Could Ask Abraham* invites students to learn timeless Jewish values through studying the stories of the Torah. With this course, students gain an understanding of biblical stories while also exploring the connection between these stories and their lives. The book, designed as a student-response journal, enriches students' Jewish identities by helping them feel like part of the Jewish people and its history, and giving them opportunities to apply Jewish values in their everyday lives.

STRUCTURE OF THE COURSE

Each chapter of *Jewish Values in Genesis: If I Could Ask Abraham* focuses on a story from Genesis and a *midah* (character trait) or a Jewish value or concept that can be learned from the story. The stories are introduced in the same order as they appear in the Bible. In the first three chapters, students are asked to look inward and explore the self, to ask, Who am I, and what is important to me? In chapters 4 through 7, the book requires students to look outward at their relationships with family and those closest to them.

Jewish Values in Genesis: If I Could Ask Abraham includes creative, interactive activities, as well as thought-provoking exercises, that integrate Jewish texts, drama, art, music, movement, and more. The Lesson Plan Manual, written as a complementary book to the student-response journal, presents teachers with fourteen ready-to-use lesson plans of approximately fifty minutes each, offering suggestions for teaching the different elements of the main text.

Every chapter in the student-response journal includes the following features:

- **Telling the Story:** a creative exploration of the biblical story.
- **Digging Deeper:** questions that help students think more deeply about the biblical story.
- **Making Meaning:** an introduction to a Jewish value or concept—identified in both Hebrew and English—and a discussion of its connection to the biblical story covered in the chapter.

Some chapters may also include:

- **Get on the Move:** a short movement-focused activity relating to the themes of the chapter.
- **Values in Action:** examples of biblical characters and people from Jewish history who demonstrated the Jewish value or concept that is the focus of the chapter.
- **What Would You Do?:** an exercise presenting examples of real-life scenarios that call for applying the Jewish value or concept that is the focus of the chapter.
- **Rabbis' Corner:** exploration of a short rabbinic text that interprets the biblical story and/or the Jewish value or concept that is the focus of the chapter.
- **Try This:** experiential prompts for activities connecting Jewish values to students' lives.
- **Torah Timeline:** summaries of stories from Genesis that are related to the theme of the chapter but are not covered in depth, presented with questions for further thought.
- **[The Jewish Value] and Me:** a journal-writing exercise to help students reflect on the relevance of the chapter's Jewish value or concept to their own lives.

USING THE LESSON PLAN MANUAL

At the start of the year, map out when you plan to teach each chapter. Before starting a new chapter with your class, read through the Lesson Plan Manual to familiarize yourself with the chapter and look at the biblical text to gain a deeper understanding of the story. You may choose to use the lessons exactly as they are, or you may decide to adapt them to fit the needs of your students. If you adapt the lessons, remember that it is important to frame your lesson around central questions and goals. This manual makes frequent references to images and activities in the student-response journal and provides the corresponding page numbers for easy reference.

Each lesson plan in the Lesson Plan Manual includes the following sections:

- **Essential Question:** an overarching question that reflects the main idea of the lesson. You might write this question on the board before class begins and refer back to it at the end of class.
- **Goals:** specific goals for each lesson corresponding to the concepts and ideas that students should understand when they complete the lesson.
- **Lesson at a Glance:** a brief overview of the lesson, including a description of the Jewish value or concept covered in the lesson and its connection to the biblical story in the chapter.
- **Materials Needed:** a list of any handouts, arts-and-crafts supplies, or other materials needed for the lesson.
- **Activities:** detailed descriptions of each activity in the lesson and a suggested time frame for each one.
- **Getting Started (in Activities):** a set induction to get students thinking about the ideas they will learn in the lesson.
- **Wrapping It Up (in Activities):** a short activity or discussion to review and reflect on the main ideas presented in the lesson.

Some lessons may also include:

- **Extension Activity:** an optional activity to enrich students' understanding of the biblical story and the Jewish value or concept covered in the lesson.
- **Resources for the Teacher:** additional background information and resources to enrich your understanding of the texts, themes, and people discussed in the chapter. All website links mentioned in this manual are hyperlinked on the course website, www.behrmanhouse.com/values-bible.

TEACHING STRATEGIES AND TIPS

Journal Writing

Each chapter of *Jewish Values in Genesis* includes open-ended questions for students to think over and write about. Through writing in their journals, students are able to reflect on the relevance of Jewish values to their lives and are encouraged to ask: Why is this Jewish value important to me, and how can I act on this value in my own life?

Whenever it is time for students to write in their journals, tell them that their writing is private and that they will not be required to share what they write with other students. At some point, students may volunteer to share some of their journal entries with the class, but this should never be mandatory.

Asking Questions

This course will likely raise questions for many students about God, the Bible, Jewish beliefs and values, and some biblical characters. Make sure that your classroom provides a safe space for students to ask questions by insisting that all the members of the classroom community—teachers and students—listen to one another with respect and sensitivity. The student-response journal provides opportunities throughout the course for students to ask questions. Encourage your class to take advantage of these opportunities and to feel comfortable asking questions at other times as well. Remind them that there are no stupid questions and that asking questions helps us learn even when we don't find answers. Explain also that asking questions about our values is a lifelong process, and our response to certain questions may change over time.

More Than One Right Answer

Throughout the student-response journal there are questions designed to help students think more deeply about the material. In many cases there is not one correct answer; rather, there are multiple interpretations of a text and a number of different ways to connect a Jewish value to our lives. The Lesson Plan Manual offers possible answers to the questions in the student-response journal so as to give the teacher some suggestions about the different directions to take the class. These answers appear in italics. Please keep in mind that they are not the only correct answers, and encourage students to be creative and to explore a broad range of possibilities.

Project-based Learning (PBL)

With project-based learning, students use the knowledge and skills they learn in class to solve real-world problems. Working alone, with a partner, or in a group, students make or develop something concrete to demonstrate what they have learned. When a class learns about Jewish values using this method of learning, students gain a deeper understanding of how these values are relevant to their lives. Classes can create their own PBL experiences, such as organizing a tzedakah or community-building project, by using many of the ideas in *Jewish Values in Genesis: If I Could Ask Abraham.* For more information on exciting activities that use project-based learning, visit www.behrmanhouse.com/project-based-learning.

At the end of the Lesson Plan Manual, you will find directions for a final project, called Bringing Torah into My Life: My Project. For the final project, students are asked to research a person from Jewish history who demonstrates one or more of the values they learned about in the course and to share what they have learned with a creative presentation in class or at an evening event for their families. See page 35 for more details.

Glossary of Hebrew Terms

Jewish Values in Genesis: If I Could Ask Abraham teaches some key Hebrew terms. Students are taught the Hebrew term for each Jewish value or concept they learn about, as well as other important Hebrew words that are scattered throughout the journal. In order to help you reinforce this vocabulary, a glossary is included in the back of this book containing all of the Hebrew terms that the students learn throughout the course. Use this glossary to play a fun game that reinforces vocabulary, for example, a memory game where students match the Hebrew word to its English translation or a competition in which teams earn points by being the first to give the correct translation of a Hebrew term.

Being Inclusive

Children vary in their learning styles. Some learn best with a hands-on approach, while others do best with a visual or auditory approach. In general, teachers who present material in a number of different ways are able to reach many more children.

Teachers of children with special needs have extra challenges. There are a broad range of cognitive, physical, and behavioral disabilities that impact learning. It is always helpful for the education director to find out from parents what kinds of accommodations are made for a special-needs child in their secular school. Below are some suggestions for teaching this course to children with learning, perceptual, or attention problems.

- For students with attention- and auditory-processing problems, teach the class in small increments and present one instruction at a time. Ask the children to repeat instructions, making sure they have processed them.
- For children with attention problems, limit teaching segments to between ten and fifteen minutes, and allow for movement between activities.
- For children who have problems with attention and/or their visual figure-ground, mask parts of the page so that they can see only the section that is being worked on.
- For children with fine-motor and handwriting problems, limit the amount of writing, drawing, and cutting required. Prepare the difficult parts of a project in advance, and have students finish the task in class. This is a good way to engage a classroom *madrich* or *madrichah*. (*The Madrichim Manual* [Behrman House] is an excellent resource for learning how to engage *madrichim* appropriately.)

Remember, the relationships you develop with your students and the relationships they build with one another are as important as the material you teach. Try to always model patience and respect for all students.

Interpersonal and Intrapersonal Learners

Some students learn best through interacting with others ("interpersonal" learners); some learn best independently ("intrapersonal" learners). With this in mind, the lesson plans in this book were written with suggestions for independent student work, as well as activities and discussions to be done with a partner, group, or whole class. In general, if the Lesson Plan Manual does not specify that students should work with a partner or in a group, you should plan for a class discussion.

Group Work

Many of the lessons in this manual include suggestions for group work. Whenever possible, plan ahead for how you want to form these groups. For some tasks you will want to group together students with a variety of talents and interests. For others you may choose to put together students with similar skills. It is important to vary the composition of your groups.

Group work is most successful when every member of the group knows his or her responsibilities. To help make a group's task (or tasks) clear, prepare written instructions before class. Many of the lesson plans in this manual include such instructions. Consider creating index cards that describe the different possible jobs. These will vary according to the type of group work. Some possible jobs are:

- Recorder—records the group's suggestions or findings.
- Reporter—reports the group's work to the class.
- Illustrator—creates an illustration of the group's ideas to be presented to the class.
- Investigator—researches to discover information.
- Encourager—encourages group members to stay on task.
- Reader—reads information to the group.

Consider laminating the job-description index cards and distributing them each time you do group work.

Integrating Technology

Your students are growing up in a world in which technology is part of their daily lives at home and at school. There are an infinite number of ways for you to take advantage of the Internet and digital applications to reinforce concepts; deepen your students' understanding of the subject matter; share what has been learned with students' families; and add creativity, interactivity, and excitement to your lessons.

Note that the Behrman House Online Learning Center offers a platform for sharing information and collaborating on projects. You can find more information about the Online Learning Center here: www.behrmanhouse.com/olc/discover-the-online-learning-center.

In addition, see below for information about the *Jewish Values in Genesis: If I Could Ask Abraham* course website.

COURSE WEBSITE

The course website, **www.behrmanhouse.com/values-bible**, provides valuable resources, including links to videos and additional reference materials, to help you enrich your students' learning experience and deepen their understanding of the biblical stories and values covered in each chapter.

For your convenience, all links to outside materials referenced in the Lesson Plan Manual are hyperlinked from the website. There is no need to retype a lengthy URL from a lesson plan. Simply visit the website and click on the links you need.

CHAPTER

1

Who Am I? Creation

Lesson 1

Essential Question: We learn from the story of the Creation of the world that all people are created in the image of God. What does this mean for how we treat others and ourselves?

Goals: In this lesson, students will:

1. Review the story of Creation using the Torah text and analyze the passages about how God created the first man and woman.
2. Define the words *b'tzelem Elohim* and explain what it means in the context of the Creation story.
3. Discuss what the idea of being created *b'tzelem Elohim* can teach us about how to treat ourselves and others.

Lesson at a Glance

In Genesis, the Torah relates that the first human being was created *b'tzelem Elohim*—"in the image of God." Being created in the image of God means that all people have Godlike qualities, such as intelligence and compassion, and that they have the capability to act like God, for instance, by helping others and improving the world around us. In this lesson, students explore what it means to be created in the image of God, using movement-based activity, textual study, and personal reflection.

Activities

1. Getting Started: Get on the Move (10 minutes)

Clear a large open space in your classroom and ask all the students to walk around the space in a natural manner. Every minute or two, tell them to stop, and then ask them to start walking again in the different ways listed in the student-response journal (as a toddler, the class bully, etc.). You may also add your own examples that you think will be fun for your class in particular, such as walking like a famous athlete or like a movie star who is popular among your students. When you ask students to walk like they were created from dust or like they were created in the image of God, they may ask you to explain what this means, but you should tell them that you will discuss what these ideas mean later. This is an exercise in improvisation, without words. There is no right or wrong way to do the activity, so students can be creative.

After you finish the exercise, ask a few students to demonstrate for the class how they walked when they were asked to walk as if they were created from dust or as if they were created in the image of God. If they wish, they can explain why they chose to walk in that specific way. Do not insist that they explain themselves, however, as the exercise is designed to give students the opportunity to express their personal interpretations through movement, and they may have difficultly expressing their interpretations in words. Other students can describe concretely what the student is doing—i.e., she is walking very upright; he is looking at the ground, etc.

2. Telling the Story (15 minutes)

The Torah tells two different stories of Creation in chapters 1 and 2 of Genesis. In this exercise, students read the narrative of God's creation of man and woman in both of these chapters. Then they fill out the chart on page 7 in pairs and answer the first question below the chart.

Note for the students that the Creation story of chapter 1 describes man and woman as having a powerful role in the world. According to this version of the story, the human being was created in the image of God and is God's partner in Creation, who rules over the land and sea. In the second chapter, man and woman are humble beings—made from dust and charged with taking care of the world rather than ruling over it. This lesson focuses on what it means to be created in the image of God (as described in Genesis 1), but it is important to keep in mind the second story of Creation as well.

Next, discuss the second question below the chart as a class.

Possible answer: *Both stories of Creation teach us important truths about what it means to be human. As humans we are powerful partners of God in fixing the world, but we are also humble creatures who are ultimately limited in what we can do to change in the world. Sometimes our task is to use nature for our own purposes, to help improve our lives and the lives of others through advancing science and technology, but at other times, our task is to take care of the Earth. Both roles are essential; we cannot ignore either one.*

3. Digging Deeper (10 minutes)

Discuss the first two questions of this exercise (on page 8) as a class. Ask the students to name some qualities of God that we also have, such as intelligence or compassion, as well as actions that God does that we can do too, such as giving food to the poor or taking care of the sick.

Possible answer to the second question: *The Torah's idea that we are all created in the image of God empowers us to help others and to do good in the world. We can learn from this idea that each one of us is important, so we should respect both ourselves and others.*

Acknowledge that although not everyone in the room may believe in God, or in a God that created the world, the Torah's story of Creation can still help us think about how we treat ourselves and others, and what our job is in the world. Whether or not one believes in God, these are important questions to ask. Also explain that those who do believe in God may have different beliefs about what God is like or whether God is all good. The student's beliefs about God will shape how he or she understands the concept of *tzelem Elohim.*

Your class may raise another interesting question: If we are created in the image of God, does that mean that *all* our traits are Godlike in some way? Or are only some of them? Encourage your class to ask these types of questions freely. Note that it is okay to leave some questions unanswered and that some of these questions are ones we may continue asking our whole lives. Ask students to independently write down their questions about God in their journals.

4. Wrapping It Up: Making Meaning (10 minutes)

Define the term *b'tzelem Elohim* as a class. Then have students do the exercise on page 9 in pairs or on their own. If there is time, students can share some of their ideas with the class.

Author's Note: The Hebrew words for *b'tzelem Elohim* are written on page 9 of the student-response journal with a dash. This was done because according to Jewish tradition, God's Hebrew name is considered holy, and after it is written down, it should not be erased or thrown out. This book places a dash in the Hebrew so as not to write God's Hebrew name in full, thereby avoiding this problem.

Extension Activity

ORDER OF CREATION: According to the Torah, God created different things on each day of Creation. In the chart below, the creations are listed in an order that is different from the one in the Torah. Reproduce the chart below and ask students to fill it out. Students should look at the first chapter of Genesis for help in filling in the right-hand column.

	On which day of creation would it make sense for this to be created?	**According to Genesis 1, on which day was this created?**
Sun, moon, and stars		
Animals and people		
Sky and sea		
Land, trees, and other plants		
Light and darkness (day and night)		
Fish and birds		

Discuss the following questions:

- What are the differences between the order students think of and the order in Genesis? What might have been the logic behind the order in Genesis?
- Why do you think that in the Creation story, man and woman were created last? Does this say anything about people's place in the world? If so, what does it say?

Remind the class that this story of Creation comes from the first chapter of Genesis, which describes people as being created in God's image, to rule over the world. In this context, one possible answer to the question of why people were created last could be: *so that they can reflect their centrality in Creation, that the world was created for them.*

Lesson 2

Essential Question: What makes each of us unique?

Goals: In this lesson, students will:

1. Study a rabbinic teaching about Creation and the uniqueness of each person.
2. Evaluate the advantages and disadvantages of each person being unique.
3. Use art to express what is unique about different people.

Lesson at a Glance

The rabbis of the Talmud teach that God creates every one of us as a unique person. This rabbinic teaching can inspire us to look inside ourselves to find the qualities that make us unique and to appreciate the unique qualities of others. This idea reminds us that we have a responsibility to contribute to the world, because the fact that every person has a unique set of abilities means that every person can impact the world in a way that no one else can. In this lesson, students not only identify their own unique qualities and those of their friends, but they must think of the unique ways they can contribute to the world around them as well.

Materials Needed

- Markers, paint, magazines, newspapers, images printed out from the computer, etc.
- Mobile devices for taking photographs or computers with Internet access to search for images
- A printer

Activities

1. Getting Started: Try This! (10 minutes)

Have the class sit in a circle, and ask each student to say something that is unique—and positive—about the person next to him or her. Alternatively, make this a written exercise: Write each student's name at the top of its own piece of paper and pass the papers around the room. Each student writes something that is unique about the classmate whose name is at the top of the paper, making sure to only write something that is positive, and then signs their name. Before passing the paper along, the student folds the paper like an accordion so that no one can see what is written other than the name at the top of the paper. This continues as the paper makes its way from student to student. At the end of the exercise, students can take home their piece of paper, with all the good qualities their classmates wrote about them.

2. Rabbis' Corner (10 minutes)

Students should complete this exercise (on page 10) in pairs. To help the class think about the question, ask: What would the world be like if everyone were the same?

Possible answer: *The pros of each person being unique can include: life is more interesting; we can learn new things from each person; I can help others with what I am good at, and they can help me with what they are good at.*

Cons could be: feeling jealous that someone has something I don't have; misunderstandings and conflicts because we want different things from our friends and express ourselves in different ways.

When they are done answering this question, ask each pair to share something they learned during their discussion that they hadn't thought about before.

3. What Makes Me Unique? (20 minutes)

Each student makes a collage on page 11 of the journal using the arts-and-crafts materials listed above. They can also take their own photos with a mobile device and create a digital collage story on Snapchat, or they can print out the photos and make a collage in their student-response journals. If there is time, students can share their collages with a partner, or a few students can volunteer to share their collages with the class.

4. Wrapping It Up: The One and Only (5 minutes)

Students write privately in their journals on page 12. If they wish, they can share what they write, or a part of what they write, with the class.

Extension Activity

TORAH TIMELINE: As a class, read the Cain and Abel story on page 13. Use the discussion questions to connect this story to the concept of being created *b'tzelem Elohim.*

CHAPTER

2

What Do I Stand For? Noah and the Flood

Lesson 1

Essential Question: What can we learn from Noah about staying true to our beliefs and values, even when others don't support us?

Goals: In this lesson, students will:

1. Analyze the story of Noah and the flood.
2. Define the term *ometz leiv* and discuss whether Noah demonstrates this quality.
3. Provide an example from their own lives of what it means to stand up for what's right.

Lesson at a Glance

When everyone else in his generation was wicked, only Noah had the strength to go against the crowd and do what was right. So when God decided to destroy the world, God chose to save Noah and his family. In this lesson, students explore the challenges that Noah and his family faced and how they overcame them. Students also discuss how they, too, can stand up for what is right in their own lives, even when others don't support them.

Materials Needed

- A long, strong rope for playing tug-of-war
- Props such as stuffed animals, a toy boat, or funny hats for acting out the story of Noah and the flood

Activities

1. Getting Started: Get on the Move (10 minutes)

Clear a large space in your classroom and play tug-of-war according to the instructions on page 14 of the student journal. If you have a small class, ask one person to switch sides after each game; if you have a large class, ask two people. After the game, discuss the questions in the journal as a class. Explain that in this lesson, the class will talk about what it means to stay true to what one believes in when everyone else is on "the other side."

2. Telling the Story (20 minutes)

Ask for volunteers to come to the front of the room and act out the conversations described on page 15 of the student journal. Use the props to make the improvisation more fun. After each conversation, invite another student to come to the front of the room to replace one of the students and act out a different conversation that could have happened. Depending on time constraints, you can choose one conversation for your students to act out, or several. Ask different students to volunteer for each conversation.

You can help students with this activity by asking questions to encourage them to imagine the conversations differently. For example: What if Noah had challenged God about building the ark? What if Noah's wife would not have wanted to go on the ark? What if Noah's neighbors had gotten angry at him for building the ark?

Remind students that there are no right or wrong answers; the Bible does not tell us about these conversations, so they are only imagining what the conversations might have been like. Explain that they are making their own midrash, a story filling in the blanks in the Bible.

After the students finish acting out the conversations, ask them to independently complete the sentence on the bottom of page 15 of their journals.

3. Digging Deeper (10 minutes)

Instruct the students to do the exercise on page 16 of their journals in pairs, and then discuss the second question as a class. This question asks students to think about how the Torah says that Noah was righteous "in his generation," and whether this description makes the students think of Noah as more or less righteous than someone who acts righteously in a generation where everyone else is righteous too?

Possible answer: *On the one hand, Noah might have been righteous only in comparison to the wickedness of everyone around him, but if you compared him to a righteous person in another generation, he would not seem nearly as righteous. On the other hand, it is much more difficult to be righteous when everyone around you is not, so in that sense, Noah was more righteous than someone who doesn't have to stand up against the crowd to do what is right.*

Ask: Is it more difficult to be righteous in a generation where everyone else is not? Why or why not?

4. Wrapping It Up: Making Meaning (10 minutes)

Define the term *ometz leiv* as a class, and discuss the first question on page 17 of the student journal. You may raise the question: Is Noah still standing up for what he believes if he is just doing what God says?

Students now answer the last two questions on page 17 privately. If there is time, they can share a part of what they write or whatever they feel comfortable sharing, in pairs.

Resources for the Teacher

For an example of another midrash on the story of Noah, visit the course website at www.behrmanhouse.com/values-bible to watch a trailer or a clip of the movie *Noah* (2014). Show this to your class, and point out what the man in the movie trailer (Anthony Hopkins) says to Noah: "I have men at my back, and you stand alone and defy me." What does this quote say about Noah?

Lesson 2

Essential Question: What makes it difficult to stay true to our beliefs, and how can we overcome these difficulties?

Goals: In this lesson, students will:

1. Learn about people throughout Jewish history who stood up for what they believed in despite what others did or said.
2. Discuss why it can be difficult to stand up for what you believe in and why people do not always do so.
3. Identify the values that are important enough to stand up for regardless of what anyone else around them says or does.

Lesson at a Glance

Throughout Jewish history, people have stood up against the crowd and done what they believed was right. In this lesson, students are split up into small groups to research some of these people and then share what they learned with the rest of the class. Students will also look inward to think about what values they are willing to stand up for in their own lives.

Materials Needed

- A computer with an Internet connection for each group
- Printouts of short biographies of each person featured in the Values in Action exercise, if Internet is not available to students (See Resources for the Teacher for where to find the printouts.)

Activities

1. Getting Started: What Would You Do? (10 minutes)

Students do the exercise on page 18 in pairs. Next, discuss the last two questions as a class. Responses to what can help you do the right thing may include: *support from your family; belief in God; or learning from role models.*

2. Values in Action (25 minutes)

Divide the class into small groups for the activity on page 19. Give each group a different person to research from this exercise. If the classroom has Internet access, ask students to research their person online. If there is no Internet access, print out a page or two describing these people's lives in advance (see Resources for the Teacher, page 11). When they are done researching/reading about their person, each group should write a short diary entry from that person's perspective. The entry should deal with the challenges that person faced and how he or she overcame them.

Explain that just as we tried to put ourselves into the shoes of Noah and his family, now we are trying to put ourselves in the shoes of other people from the Bible and Jewish history to understand the challenges they faced and how they overcame them. If there is time, groups should share their diary entries with the class.

3. Staying True to My Values (10 minutes)

As a class, do some brainstorming to create a list of values, and then write the list on the board. Each student now chooses the values that are most important to him or her and writes about them in the student-response journal, on page 21. If there is time, ask students to divide themselves into pairs to share the values they chose, as well as the reasons for their choices, with their partner.

4. Wrapping It Up: Try This! (5 minutes)

Encourage students to do this assignment (page 21) at home. Ask them to prepare a presentation about the values that are important to their families. Or, if this assignment is not realistic for your class, ask them to write down the values their families choose and report back to the class. They should make a chart with two columns. In one column they should put the name of each family member they intend to ask, and then they should leave the second column blank to write in the values that family member chooses.

Extension Activity

TORAH TIMELINE (PAGE 22): Students should read the story of the Tower of Babel (Genesis 11:1–8) and answer the questions in the journal in pairs or as a class. This is a difficult story with many possible interpretations. It is not clear what (if anything) is wrong with building a tower that reaches the sky or why God is upset that "nothing they plan to do will be out of their reach." The Midrash gives a powerful interpretation of the story, suggesting that everyone building the tower was so united in working toward their goal that they stopped caring about individual people. They became a totalitarian society, and no one seems to have protested. Not only do they speak one language literally, but, according to the Midrash, they are also of "one speech," in complete agreement with one another. With this midrash, the rabbis critique the model of society in which everyone does the same thing. They show us the dangers of what happens when there is no Noah to stand up against the crowd and say, "This is wrong."

Resources for the Teacher

For information on the people in the Values in Action exercise, visit the course website at http://www.behrmanhouse.com/values-bible and see the following sources:

- Exodus 2:1–10 (Pharaoh's daughter)
- Numbers 13:1–33 and 14:1–10 (Caleb and Joshua)

Also visit the course website for more information on Midrash and a more in-depth interpretation of the Tower of Babel story.

CHAPTER

3

Where Do I Find Faith and Hope? Abraham and Sarah

Lesson 1

Essential Question: How can the story of Abraham and Sarah going to Canaan inspire us to have faith to take risks and make changes in our lives?

Goals: In this lesson, students will:

1. Analyze the story of *Lech Lecha*, in which Abram and Sarai (later known as Abraham and Sarah) go to Canaan.
2. Define the word *bitachon* (trust or faith).
3. Explain how having trust in God helps Abram and Sarai find the strength to leave their home for an unknown place that God will show them.

Lesson at a Glance

When God instructs Abram to leave his native land and go to a land that God would show him, Abram and Sarai get up and go. They leave behind everything they know—land, family, culture—and head toward a land they know nothing about, not even its name or location. This act takes tremendous *bitachon*, or trust, in God. In this lesson, students explore Abram and Sarai's journey in depth and reflect on journeys in their lives and their families' lives.

Materials Needed

- A large map of modern Israel that identifies major cities (You can bring in an actual map or project a map from your computer onto the SMART Board.)
- Masking tape (optional)

Activities

1. Getting Started: Doing Something New (5 minutes)

Students should do the exercise on page 23 of the journal, which asks them to write about a time they tried something new and the challenges involved in doing so. Those who wish to can share their experiences with the class.

2. Telling the Story (15 minutes)

In pairs, students should do the exercise on pages 24–25. If possible, bring a big map of Israel to class to show students where each place in the story is located in relation to modern-day places.

Alternatively, use masking tape to make an outline of Canaan on the floor of your classroom. Tell the students to read the text in pairs, and then ask them to "walk" the same path as Abram and Sarai in the marked-off area. To do this they must first identify where Haran is (approximately) in relation to Canaan and then mark the location on the floor by making an X with the masking tape. Next they should put down Xs for Shechem, Bethel, and the Negev, and then walk from place to place according to Abram and Sarai's route.

3. Digging Deeper (10 minutes)

As a class, answer the questions on page 26. Possible answers include:

1) *"From your land, from your birthplace, from your family's home" emphasizes how difficult it is for Abram and Sarai to leave Haran—not only do they leave their land, they also leave the place where they were born and where their families are.*

2) *Going to "the land that I [God] will show you," knowing nothing about the destination, requires more trust in God than going to a place that God has named and that you know something about.*

3) *We see from this story that Abram and Sarai have trust in God and are willing to take risks to start a new life.*

Other questions to consider: What does God mean when God says that Abram will "be a blessing"? Why does Abram build altars to God throughout his journey?

4. Stepping into Their Sandals (10 minutes)

Students should work on this exercise (page 27) independently. If there is time, they can share what they have written with a classmate. Tell the students that one student in the pair should read one of the text messages, and the other student should respond by saying what he or she would write back.

5. Making Meaning (5 minutes)

On page 28 of the student-response journal, students define *bitachon* and together explore its role in the *Lech Lecha* story.

6. Wrapping It Up: Try This! Part I (5 minutes)

Encourage the students to interview a family member as a homework assignment (as described on page 29). Ask them to answer the following questions in writing or in class discussion: Who will you interview? What questions will you ask them?

They can write down what the family member tells them and find related family photos. Students can share their family stories in the next class.

Resources for the Teacher

For a map of modern-day Israel and the Israeli-controlled territories, see the course website at www.behrmanhouse.com/values-bible. You can use this map to show students the geography of Israel and the surrounding region. Point out Jerusalem, Tel Aviv, and Beersheba, as well as the Negev region. You can also show students where Shechem and Bethel are located. Explain that in English, Shechem is often called Nablus, which is the Arabic name for the city.

For more information on Haran, which is believed to be the same city as today's Harran in modern-day Turkey, see www.behrmanhouse.com/values-bible. Show students the map on this site. Emphasize how long it would take to walk from Haran to Shechem—it's around a 400-mile walk! You can also explain that Abram actually began his journey in Ur, in modern day Iraq, before he moved with his father's household to Haran. The journey from Ur to Canaan via Haran was 955 miles. See www.behrmanhouse.com/values-bible.

Lesson 2

Essential Question: What gives us the strength to try something new, to make our lives or the world better?

Goals: In this lesson, students will:

1. Discuss what gives them the strength to take risks and make changes.
2. Identify people throughout Jewish history who found the faith to take risks and make changes in their lives and the world.
3. Choose one new thing they would like to do, or identify a change they would like to make in their lives.

Lesson at a Glance

Throughout Jewish history, people have followed in Abraham and Sarah's footsteps by going on physical, emotional, and spiritual journeys. Many have left the familiar behind for the unknown, in the hopes of a better future. In this lesson, students learn more about such people in Jewish history and try to understand the *bitachon* that gave them strength on their journeys. Students also try to identify their own sources of strength, which can help them go forward to try new things and make changes in their lives.

Materials Needed

- Computers with Internet access or handouts about each of the people featured in the Values in Action exercise

Activities

1. Getting Started: Singing Together (10 minutes)

Students sing Debbie Friedman's "L'chi Lach" together. As a class, discuss the song's meaning by using the guiding questions on page 29 of the student journal. Explain how a journey can be something physical, such as moving to a new place, or a process of spiritual, psychological, or emotional change that does not require a physical effort.

Links to the song and lyrics are available at www.behrmanhouse.com/values-bible.

2. Values in Action (15 minutes)

In pairs (or small groups), students should complete the exercise on journal pages 30–31. Each pair is assigned a different person, or group of people, to write about and then shares what they wrote with the class. If there is time, ask students to read more about these people on the Internet or in handouts.

Alternatively, ask students to write an imaginary letter from the person they researched to another student in the class or to a younger family member. In the letter, the person should recall what gave him or her *bitachon* to accomplish what they did and encourage the recipient of the letter to find the *bitachon* to do what they dream of doing.

3. Try This! Part II (15 minutes)

Ask for a few volunteers to share their family stories with the class and answer the following question: What was the "journey" your family members went on? What do you think gave them the strength to do what they did?

4. Wrapping It Up: *Bitachon* and Me (10 minutes)

Students complete the exercise on page 32 individually. If there is time, they can share part of what they wrote in pairs.

Extension Activity

TORAH TIMELINE (PAGE 33): Students read and explore the stories of Sodom and Gomorrah and the binding of Isaac using the discussion questions in the student journal. The story of God asking Abraham to sacrifice Isaac is one of the most difficult stories in all of the Bible. How could God ask Abraham to do such a morally reprehensible act? Commentators on the Bible have struggled with it for at least as long as people have been writing biblical commentaries. It is important to keep in mind that in the end, God stopped Abraham from killing Isaac. Many would argue that God never actually wanted Abraham to kill his son. But the question remains, why would God ask Abraham to do such a thing?

Some commentators say that God was testing Abraham to see if he was willing to trust God over his own understanding of what is right. Others say that when keeping in mind that child sacrifice was common at the time, one could say that the real test was not whether Abraham was willing to sacrifice Isaac, but whether he was willing to stop himself from sacrificing Isaac once the angel told him to stop. Elie Wiesel argues that with this commandment, God was not just testing Abraham; Abraham was testing God to see whether God would actually require him to perform child sacrifice.

The juxtaposition of the story of Sodom and Gomorrah with the binding of Isaac raises even more questions. Why did Abraham argue with God to save the innocent people of Sodom and Gomorrah but not his own son? Some explain that if you look closely at the story of Sodom and Gomorrah, you will notice that God never tells Abraham that God is going to destroy the cities, and therefore Abraham's protests are about something he thinks God has not already decided upon.

Ask students for their interpretations of the stories, and offer some of your own. Emphasize again that it is okay if we do not have all the answers to our questions; asking questions is a lifelong process. For more interpretations of these stories, see Resources for the Teacher, below, and www.behrmanhouse.com/values-bible.

Resources for the Teacher

For information to hand out to your students regarding the people in the Values in Action exercise and for more interpretations of the binding of Isaac, see www.behrmanhouse.com/values-bible. For the story of the Israelites crossing the Sea of Reeds, see also Exodus 14.

CHAPTER

4

How Can I Pay It Forward? Rebekah at the Well

Lesson 1

Essential Question: How can the story of Rebekah at the well inspire us to act with kindness within our families?

Goals: In this lesson, students will:

1. Analyze the story of Rebekah at the well.
2. Define *chesed* (kindness) and explain how Rebekah demonstrates *chesed* at the well.
3. Discuss why *chesed* matters and how it helps us become the best people and the best families we can be.

Lesson at a Glance

When Abraham sent his servant Eliezer to find a wife for his son Isaac, Eliezer had to figure out which *midot* (character traits) to look for in the woman who would become part of the Jewish people's "first family." In this lesson, students create their own comic strips to illustrate the story of Eliezer meeting Rebekah, Isaac's future wife. They also debate which midot are the most important in a family member and discuss why Eliezer chose *chesed* (kindness) as the *midah* to look for.

Materials Needed

- Colored pencils, markers, and/or crayons

Activities

1. Getting Started: What Would You Look For? (10 minutes)

On page 34 of the journal, each student makes a list of the three most important *midot* in a family member. Then, as a class, try to come up with what your class thinks are the three most important *midot* in a family member by debating and voting on the options.

2. Telling the Story (15 minutes)

Students read the story of Rebekah at the well independently (pages 35–36 in the student-response journal) and then, in the space allotted in their journals, draw their own comic strips illustrating different parts of the story. Suggest that they add thought bubbles to the comics to show the characters' thoughts and feelings. If there is extra time, students can look at each other's comics when they are done with their own.

3. Digging Deeper (10 minutes)

Begin by asking students to answer the first three questions on page 37 in pairs.

Possible answers to the first three questions:

1) *Rebekah could have responded by saying, "I am sorry, I told my father I would be right back with the water, so I have to hurry"; by giving Eliezer something to drink but not his camels; by giving Eliezer and his camels the water from her pitcher but not refilling her pitcher and giving them more.*

2) *Rebekah may have chosen to go to such extremes to help a stranger simply because she saw he was in a tough situation, empathized with him, and wanted to help as much as she could. Maybe she imagined herself in his place and acted as she would have wanted someone to act toward her.*

3) *Rebekah's choice shows how she went far beyond what would be expected in being kind to a stranger. She could have drawn the line at any number of places, and said, "I will be kind to this point and no further—I also have to worry about myself and my family," but instead she gave as much as possible.*

Then discuss the last question as a class: Do you think Eliezer came up with a good way to test Rebekah's character? Why or why not? If the students see kindness as the most important quality in a family member, then Eliezer's test was an excellent one. If they see another quality (such as loyalty to family) as being the most important, then this was not the best test.

4. Making Meaning (10 minutes)

Define *chesed* as a class. Students should then independently answer the questions on page 38 of their journals. If there is time, they can share their answers with a partner.

5. Wrapping It Up: Try This! (5 minutes)

Invite students to do the exercise on page 38 at home with their family and report back to the class about what their families came up with. Ask students to make a chart to show the class the different opinions of their family members. The chart should have one column for the names of their family members and another for the *midah* each person in the family chooses. Below the chart, the student should write down the test their family makes up.

Lesson 2

Essential Question: How can we do acts of *chesed* (kindness) in our everyday lives?

Goals: In this lesson, students will:

1. Give examples of acts of *chesed* in their everyday lives.
2. Plan a "Pay It Forward Day" to encourage acts of *chesed* in their community.
3. Discuss how they expect the people for whom they do *chesed* to behave and how these expectations influence the way they (the students) act.

Lesson at a Glance

There are countless opportunities for us to do acts of kindness in our everyday lives—whether those acts are small or big, easy or difficult. Like Rebekah, we just need to take advantage of those opportunities. The effects of one small act of kindness can be far greater than we ever expected, as the recipient of our kindness will likely be kind to another person, who will be kind to another person, and so forth, in a ripple effect. In this lesson, students explore how they can do more acts of kindness in their everyday lives and plan a "Pay It Forward Day" to inspire acts of kindness in their community.

Materials Needed

- "Pay It Forward" cards or bracelets (You can make or print the cards yourself, or you can order the bracelets. Go to www.behrmanhouse.com/values-bible for ordering information.)

Activities

1. Getting Started: Get on the Move (10 minutes)

Play the game on page 39 of the student journal to get your class thinking about how acts of kindness (or the opposite) can have a ripple effect. In this game, everyone sits in a circle with their eyes closed. One student is chosen to begin the game and taps the person in the next seat, who should then open his or her eyes. The first student makes a face for the second student, expressing a specific emotion. The second student repeats the process, tapping the student next to him or her. Each student tries to make the exact same face as the previous student, and the game continues until everyone has had a turn. At the end, the last student makes the face for the first student. In this way, the students have "passed along" this emotion to the entire circle. So too, when we do a kindness for someone, the kindness inspires others to be kind, which then inspires the people around *them* to be kind, and so on.

When the game is over, discuss the questions in the student-response journal with your class.

2. *Chesed* Hero (10 minutes)

In pairs, students review the story of Ruth (page 40) and answer the questions. Discuss the last question together as a class.

3. Everyday Acts of Kindness (5 minutes)

In small groups, students brainstorm to come up with small acts of kindness that can be done at school and at home. They should record their ideas on page 41 of their journals. Each student then chooses one of these acts of kindness to do the following week and shares what he or she has chosen with the group.

4. Try This! (15 minutes)

Plan a "Pay It Forward Day" for your school or synagogue:

- As a class, brainstorm to make a list of acts of kindness that students are able to do that day. Examples include: carrying someone's books for them; bringing a teacher a cup of water; making cards for the school staff thanking them for what they do to make the school run smoothly; or making care packages for children who are sick at home.
- In addition to doing spontaneous acts of kindness, your class can plan more ambitious *chesed* projects for the Pay It Forward Day. If relevant, break the students into small groups and ask each group to plan a different project.
- Make simple Pay It Forward cards (for example, by writing "Pay It Forward" on index cards); print out Pay It Forward cards from the Internet; or give out Pay It Forward bracelets (go to the course website at www.behrmanhouse.com/values-bible for ordering information).
- In consultation with your school administration, choose a date for the Pay It Forward Day.

After Pay It Forward Day is over, ask students to reflect on the experience in their journals (on page 42). Those who wish to can share their reflections with the class.

5. Wrapping It Up: What Do I Get in Return? (10 minutes)

Students answer the questions on page 43 individually. If there is time, they can share some of their answers with another student or the entire class.

Extension Activity

SHOULD I STAY OR SHOULD I GO?: Basing their skit on Ruth 1:6–18, students act out the dialogue between Naomi and her daughters-in-law that takes place when Naomi leaves Moab for the Land of Israel. Students also act out what they imagine Ruth and Orpah were thinking as they decided whether or not to go with Naomi.

Resources for the Teacher

For additional Pay It Forward resources, visit www.behrmanhouse.com/values-bible.

CHAPTER

5

Should I Always Tell the Truth? Jacob and Esau

Lesson 1

Essential Question: How does Jacob's decision to lie shape what happens to him, and what can we learn from his experiences?

Goals: In this lesson, students will:

1. Analyze the story of Jacob taking Esau's blessing.
2. Debate whether Jacob is justified in not telling the truth in this situation.
3. Define *emet* (truth) and identify the consequences of not telling the truth.

Lesson at a Glance

Based on his mother's advice, Jacob chooses to lie to his father in order to receive the blessing for the firstborn, which Isaac intends to give Esau. In this lesson, students examine Jacob's motivations for this choice and the impact of his decision on his life and family. They also explore what we can learn from Jacob about how our choices to tell the truth or to lie can shape our relationships and the world around us.

Materials Needed

- Props to act out the story of Jacob and Esau's blessing (optional)
- Markers, crayons, or colored pencils (optional)

Activities

1. Getting Started: Two Truths and a Lie (10 minutes)

Play the game on page 44 as a class. Students take turns telling two truths and one lie, while the rest of the class guesses which statements are true and which is not. When the game is over, students respond to the prompts in the journal.

2. Telling the Story (10 minutes)

Students use the script on pages 45–46 to act out the story of Jacob taking Esau's blessing.

Suggestions to enrich the skit:

- At different points in the story, freeze the scene and ask the audience to say what the different characters are feeling.
- Bring in props, such as food and a piece of soft "furry" fabric for Jacob to put on his arm.

3. Digging Deeper (20 minutes)

Discuss the first question on page 47 as a class.

Possible answer: *Jacob wants to get the blessing for the firstborn, to be blessed with being master of his brother. (The Bible goes into more detail about this blessing in Genesis 27:28–29.) Rebekah knows that Jacob is destined to be the master of his brother on account of her prophecy when she was pregnant, and she presumably believes that God intends for Jacob to receive the blessing. At stake may also be the future of the Jewish people—who will inherit Abraham's special covenant with God?*

Divide students into three groups: the prosecution, the defense, and the judges (the judges group may be smaller than the other two), and put Jacob on trial for unfairly "stealing" Esau's blessing. The prosecution and defense prepare their arguments, and the judges prepare questions to ask the two sides. Then stage the trial. If there is only a short time available, each side presents a two-minute argument, and the judges make a ruling. If there is more time, each side can call witnesses to the stand, such as Rebekah, Isaac, and Esau, and present a counterargument.

Defense arguments may include: *Esau doesn't deserve the blessing and may use the power given in the blessing unwisely; Esau already demonstrated that he doesn't care about the birthright when he sold his birthright for soup; Jacob is listening to his mother; Jacob will use the privileges of the blessing for good; Jacob's future descendants deserve this blessing; Jacob is fulfilling his mother's prophecy that his younger brother will serve the older brother, etc.*

Prosecutor's arguments may include: *Jacob lied to his father; Jacob disrespected his father's wishes to bless Esau; it's not fair to Esau; just because Rebekah told Jacob to take the blessing doesn't mean that he should have listened; the ends (that the person who is most deserving of the blessing gets the blessing) don't justify the means, etc.*

The judges then decide whether Jacob is guilty or innocent and what his punishment should be, if any. As a class, vote on whether you agree with the judge.

Discuss the last question together. Point out that for some, the very idea of this trial might be difficult, because it allows for the possibility that Jacob, our forefather, made a mistake. But we can also see the mistakes of characters in the Bible as a learning opportunity for us. Biblical characters, like us, were imperfect human beings, and we can learn not only from their good choices but also from their bad choices.

This mock trial raises the question: Was Jacob punished for his dishonesty? On the one hand, he was forced to run away from home to Haran, where his uncle Laban tricked him by giving him Leah as a wife instead of his beloved, Rachel. But, on the other hand, in Haran Jacob ultimately had a large family, becoming one of the forefathers of the Jewish people, and his descendants inherited the blessing of the firstborn rather than Esau's descendants. The students will revisit the question of whether Jacob was punished in the next lesson, when they discuss Laban's trickery. This discussion also raises another important question: Are people always punished for what they do wrong? Why or why not?

4. Wrapping It Up: Making Meaning (10 minutes)

Define the value of *emet* as a class, and then ask the students to complete the exercise on page 48 individually. If they run out of time, students can complete the drawing at home. At the end of this class or at the beginning of the next, students share their drawings with a partner.

Resources for the Teacher

On learning from the mistakes of biblical characters, see www.behrmanhouse.com/values-bible.

Lesson 2

Essential Question: Is it ever okay to lie? If so, when and why?

Goals: In this lesson, students will:

1. Analyze the story of Laban tricking Jacob by giving him Leah as a wife instead of Rachel.
2. Study a rabbinic commentary on this story.
3. Provide examples from their own lives of times when they had to make difficult choices about whether or not to tell the truth.

Lesson at a Glance

Jacob's choice to lie to his father by pretending to be Esau not only shaped Jacob's life and the life of his immediate family, but it changed the course of Jewish history. Because of Isaac's blessing, Jacob became one of the forefathers of the Jewish people. In this lesson, students examine how certain crucial choices about whether or not to tell the truth reverberate throughout Jewish history. They reflect on their own choices about telling the truth and how those choices have affected their lives and impacted others. This self-reflection will help students understand the complexity of ethical choices, as they question whether the simple guideline of "tell the truth" applies in all contexts.

Activities

1. Getting Started: What Would You Do? (10 minutes)

As a class, students vote on whether or not to tell the truth in each scenario described on page 49 of the student-response journal, with one or two students arguing in favor of each side before the vote. If there is time, invite pairs of students to the front of the room to act out the situations and share their responses.

2. Torah Timeline (10 minutes)

In pairs, students read the story on page 50 and answer the questions.

This story may raise questions. First, why didn't Jacob realize that he had married Leah and not Rachel? According to the rabbis of the Talmud, Jacob and Rachel anticipated that Laban might try to trick Jacob, and they agreed on secret signs so that he would know it was her. But when the night of the wedding approached, Rachel did not want Leah to be ashamed, so she taught Leah the secret signs (Bava Batra 123a).

This rabbinical story does not answer all our questions. Why didn't Jacob realize that he married Leah until the morning? Did they not talk at night, after the wedding? Also, teaching Leah the secret signs only pushed off Leah's embarrassment to the following morning, when Jacob saw it was her. These are good questions, and the midrash shows that the rabbis struggled with them too.

Students may also ask why Jacob was allowed to marry two women. Explain that in ancient times, a man was permitted to marry more than one woman. The prohibition against polygamy in Judaism was only established around a thousand years ago (and even then, the prohibition was not accepted by all Jewish communities worldwide—Yemenite Jewish men could have more than one wife until modern times and only stopped when they came to Israel). The Bible does make it clear, however, that marrying more than one woman often leads to trouble. We see this not only in the story here, but in other biblical stories as well (such as the tale of Abraham, Sarah, and Hagar).

3. Rabbis' Corner (10 minutes)

As a class, read the midrash on page 51 and answer the questions that follow.

4. Choices (15 minutes)

Complete the exercise on pages 52–53 as a class. For each choice, invite one student to suggest a different choice than the one the class decides on. Ask the class how the story would have played out differently had that been the choice. Invite another student to give the logical consequence of the alternate choice, and then ask a third student to continue the story chain from there. You can make as many story chains as you wish, using as many alternative choices as the students can come up with.

Point out to your class that just as we saw that doing kindness has a ripple effect, so too other ethical choices can have repercussions far beyond what is immediately apparent. A single choice to tell the truth or to lie can shape the lives of future generations.

5. Wrapping It Up: *Emet* and Me (5 minutes)

Students answer the questions on page 54 individually. If there is time, students can share with a partner one example of honesty or dishonesty in their lives and the consequences of the decision. Or, discuss the last question on page 54 as a class.

CHAPTER

6

What Can I Do about Feeling Jealous? Joseph and His Brothers

Lesson 1

Essential Question: What can we learn from the story of Joseph and his brothers about the causes and consequences of jealousy?

Goals: In this lesson, students will:

1. Analyze the story of Joseph and his brothers.
2. Identify the different actions that led to the ending of the story and imagine what each of the characters could have done differently to avoid this chain of events.
3. Discuss what we can learn from the mistakes people make in this story.

Lesson at a Glance

When Jacob openly favors his son Joseph, the rest of Jacob's sons become jealous of their brother. This jealousy ultimately leads to Joseph being sold into slavery. In this lesson, students examine the different choices leading up to this tragedy. They explore how jealousy can destroy a family and what could have been done differently in this story to avoid a tragic outcome. The lesson shows how a number of different ethical choices may intersect with one another and that often, many people share responsibility for something that happens. Students also learn that we are not only responsible for how we act when we are jealous, but for what we do to cause jealousy in others and how we respond to those who are jealous of us.

Materials Needed

- A computer and projector for playing a video clip

Activities

1. Getting Started: Get on the Move (10 minutes)

Clear a large space in the middle of the classroom, and ask the students whose birthdays are on an even day of the month to play freeze tag. Tell the other students that while their classmates are playing, they must sit at their desks and do a short written assignment. When the game is over, discuss the second question on page 55 of the journal as a class. Then ask students to individually answer the third question in writing.

2. Telling the Story (10 minutes)

Students learn the story of Joseph and his brothers by filling in the thought bubbles on pages 56–57. This exercise is done in pairs.

3. Write Your Own Midrash (15 minutes)

Show your class the first five and a half minutes of the DreamWorks' film *Joseph: King of Dreams.* (A link to the video clip is available at www.behrmanhouse.com/values-bible.) Explain that most of the story in the video is midrash, which fills in the blanks of the Bible's narrative, and that the Torah only tells the story of Joseph's birth in just three verses (Genesis 30:22–24) and does not mention Joseph again until chapter 37, when he is seventeen.

After watching the video clip, students do the exercise on page 58 individually. If they would like to, they can share their poem or story with the class.

4. Whose Fault Is It? (10 minutes)

Read the captions on pages 56–57 out loud to the class. Ask students to stand up when you reach a point in the story where they think a character does something that affects the story's chain of events. At the end of the story, students fill out the chart on page 59, on their own or in pairs.

5. Wrapping It Up (5 minutes)

To conclude the lesson, discuss the last question in the Whose Fault Is It? exercise as a class. Encourage students to give concrete examples about how they can apply these lessons to their own lives.

Extension Activity

MIDRASH MAKING: Before you show the video clip for the Write Your Own Midrash exercise on page 58, ask students to read the relevant verses from the Bible (Genesis 30:22–24), and point out that the Bible does not mention Joseph again until he is seventeen. Ask students to make a chart—with one side for listing all of the things in the movie clip that are mentioned in the Bible and the other side for listing the events in the clip that are not—and ask them to fill it out while they watch the video.

Discuss the following questions as a class:

What kinds of things does the movie add that are not in the Bible? Possible answers include: *conversations, feelings, and some events (such as Joseph building the irrigation route and spearing the fish).*

Why does the movie add these details? Possible answers include: *to make the story more real; to help us empathize with the characters.*

How do you think the moviemakers decided what to add? Possible answers include: *They wanted to explain why characters do what they do; to teach us a lesson about our lives; or to entertain us.*

Explain that a midrash fills in the gaps in biblical stories, like the story they read earlier about Jacob and Leah's conversation the morning after their wedding. When they filled in the thought bubbles in the exercise above, they actually made a kind of midrash.

For further enrichment, students can compare and contrast this movie with *Joseph and the Amazing Technicolor Dreamcoat* (find a link at www.behrmanhouse.com/values-bible) to see how different filmmakers interpret the story differently, making different *midrashim.*

Lesson 2

Essential Question: How can we avoid acting out of jealousy?

Goals: In this lesson, students will:

1. Define *kinah* (jealousy) and give concrete examples of it from their own lives.
2. Do an artistic project to express what they appreciate in their own lives.
3. Identify ways to avoid acting on jealousy, particularly among family.

Lesson at a Glance

Everyone feels jealous sometimes. The challenge, however, is what we do when we feel jealous or when someone feels jealous of us. Our choices determine whether or not those feelings are destructive to our relationships. In this lesson, students explore different ways to avoid acting out of jealousy, learning from Joseph and his family's mistakes. They study a teaching from the rabbis about the importance of appreciating the blessings in one's life and consider how this way of thinking can help them avoid feelings of jealousy.

Materials Needed

- Markers, colored pencils, and/or crayons
- Poster board and construction paper in different colors (optional)

Activities

1. Getting Started: Making Meaning (10 minutes)

Define the concept of *kinah* (jealousy) as a class, and then have the students individually complete the exercise on page 60. Those who wish to can share one of their answers with the class.

2. Rabbis' Corner (20 minutes)

As a class, brainstorm different ways to stop yourself from acting out of jealousy (possible answers: *talk with someone you trust about your jealous feelings; write in a journal about your feelings instead of acting on them*) and how to avoid causing others to be jealous (possible answers: *don't brag; don't play favorites*). Hint: Think about what Joseph and his family could have done differently to avoid what happened.

Read the quote from *Pirkei Avot* on page 61 as a class, and ask: How can appreciating what we have help us to avoid jealousy? Explain the Coat of Many Colors project. There are several options for how to do this project, depending on time and resources:

Option #1: Each student draws in the student journal.

Option #2: Each student receives a piece of poster board cut into the shape of a coat and glues pieces of construction paper onto it. On each colored piece, students write or draw about something they appreciate in their lives. When they finish their projects, they can go around and look at other students' collages.

In either of these options, students can do the project in pairs.

Option #3: Make a coat as a class, with one big poster board. Each student or pair of students gets a strip of construction paper and writes or draws something on it that they appreciate. Then they glue the strips onto the poster-board coat and hang it in the classroom.

3. Torah Timeline (15 minutes)

Students answer the questions on page 63 in pairs. Discuss the last two questions as a class.

4. Wrapping It Up: Jealousy in the Family (5 minutes)

Discuss the first question on page 62 as a class using Joseph's family as an example. Then invite the students to complete the second question with their families, building on the brainstorming session they had in class. Encourage students to add suggestions that were not discussed in class and to make the suggestions as concrete as possible. Students report one new idea their families came up with in the next class.

CHAPTER

7

How Can I Take Responsibility? Judah and Benjamin

Lesson 1

Essential Question: What can we learn from the story of Judah and Benjamin about taking responsibility for others?

Goals: In this lesson, students will:

1. Explain how Judah took responsibility for protecting Benjamin.
2. Imagine the motivations of the different characters in the story.
3. Learn about the concept of *acharayut* (responsibility) and discuss why taking responsibility is important in our lives.

Lesson at a Glance

When Judah insists that he be taken as a servant instead of his brother Benjamin, we see how much he has changed since Joseph was sold into slavery. Judah takes responsibility for protecting his brother as he promised his father he would. In this lesson, students explore the value of taking responsibility by putting themselves in the shoes of the different members of Joseph's family and learning from the story of Judah and Benjamin about the importance of taking responsibility in their own lives.

Materials Needed

- Blindfolds for each pair of students (An old T-shirt, handkerchief, or scarf works fine.)
- Objects to serve as obstacles during the game. These can be things you have around the classroom, such as chairs, books, etc. (optional)
- Mobile devices for taking videos (optional)

Activities

1. Getting Started: Get on the Move (15 minutes)

Create a large open area in the classroom (if possible, go outside or move to a larger room). If you wish, place a few obstacles around the open area, such as chairs or books. Divide students into pairs, and give one person in each pair a blindfold to wear. The other person in the pair guides his partner around the room, without talking. Then the pair switches roles. If possible, play music while the students are walking around.

When the game is done, students write their responses to the experience in their journals, on page 64. Ask a few students to share with the class whether they preferred leading or being led and why they feel this way.

2. Telling the Story (20 minutes)

Begin by asking the students to read the newspaper article on page 65 on their own. Then divide the class into groups of four, with one student acting as the interviewer; another as Judah; another, Joseph; and the fourth, all the other brothers. Students act out the interview, imagining how each person would answer the interviewer's questions. They may also add a few questions of their own to the interview and respond to them. If possible, have the students take a video of their interviews.

Alternatively (particularly if you have a small class), do the exercise as a class, with four student volunteers acting out the interview for the rest of the class.

3. Making Meaning (10 minutes)

Students should answer the questions on page 67 in pairs.

Discuss the third question as a class. Possible response: *As a result of Joseph taking responsibility for saving his family (by inviting them to live with him in Egypt), his family not only survives the famine, but they also stay together as a family, eventually becoming a large nation. Whereas in the generations before Joseph and his brothers only one son inherited the covenant of Abraham and the other son became the forefather of a different nation (Isaac and Ishmael, Jacob and Esau), in this generation, all twelve sons inherit the covenant of Abraham and pass it on to their children, who are all part of the Jewish people.*

On the other hand, as a result of Jacob and his family going down to Egypt, the Jewish people end up staying in Egypt for hundreds of years and becoming slaves there. Although God did tell Abraham that his children would one day be slaves, this "detour" in Egypt demonstrates that taking responsibility sometimes involves challenges and setbacks, as the Jewish people ultimately go on to be redeemed from Egypt, receive the Torah, and return to the Land of Israel.

Discuss question 4 as well. Ask the class: What would happen in a world where no one took responsibility?

4. Wrapping It Up: Try This! (5 minutes)

Invite your students, together with their families, to decide on a family project that requires taking responsibility, as described on page 67. Students should report back to the class about the project their family chooses.

Alternatively, students can choose a class project that involves taking responsibility, such as committing to regularly clean up the school yard, or developing a buddy project to help younger students.

Lesson 2

Essential Question: What are the challenges of responsibility and how can we overcome them?

Goals: In this lesson, students will:

1. Give examples from the Bible and Jewish history of people taking responsibility.
2. Identify the challenges of taking responsibility and ways of dealing with those challenges.
3. Commit to taking on a new responsibility in their lives.

Lesson at a Glance

Throughout the Bible and Jewish history, people have stepped up and taken responsibility for others, even at great risk to themselves. In this lesson, students explore the idea of taking responsibility and the challenges involved in it. They also make concrete resolutions regarding how they can take on more responsibility in their own lives.

Materials Needed

- Props for role-playing, such as a baby doll, a toy bow-and-arrow set, a crown, etc. (optional)
- A large poster board and multicolored index cards or strips of paper for each student (optional)

Activities

1. Getting Started: What Would You Do? (15 minutes)

Students begin by independently answering all parts of the first question on page 68 of the student journal. Then invite four students to act out the scene described in the exercise—one student should play the younger brother; another should act out what the older sibling says; and another should act out what the older sibling really feels; and a fourth student should play the mother. Then discuss both parts of the second question on page 68 as a class.

2. Values in Action (25 minutes)

Students complete the exercise on pages 69–70 in small groups. Each group is assigned one of the people described in the exercise. (If there is time, they can also read about the person on the Internet or in books available in the classroom.) One representative from each group then presents to the class by role-playing as the person they studied. Using first-person language (like "I" and "me"), the student answers the questions in the student journal as they imagine the person would.

Optional: Bring in some props for the role-play, such as a baby doll, a toy bow-and-arrow set, a crown, etc. Or bring in a variety of seemingly unrelated objects and challenge the students to use them in their role-playing.

3. Wrapping It Up: *Acharayut* and Me (10 minutes)

Students answer the questions on page 70 independently. Those who wish to can share their answers with the class.

Optional: Give each student a small strip of paper or an index card (try to make them different colors). Based on what they write in their journals, each student writes down one resolution, completing the sentence, "I will take responsibility by . . . " Students can choose whether or not to write their names next to their resolutions. Then make a large poster to hang in the classroom, putting "I will take responsibility by . . . " at the top. Paste the students' resolutions on the poster.

Resources for the Teacher

For information to print out about each person/group of people in the Values in Action exercise, see the course website and the following biblical sources:

- Miriam: Exodus 2:1–9
- The two and a half tribes who did not enter the Land of Israel: Numbers 32:1–25
- Esther: Esther 3:12–15, 4:1–17

Bringing Torah into My Life: My Project

Introducing the Project

Introduce this project by explaining to the students that their families and/or other students in the school would like to learn about the importance of Jewish values in history and today. With this project, the students' task is to share what they have learned in this course about how Jewish values from the Bible have guided people throughout Jewish history and how they continue to guide us today.

You can choose to introduce this project early on (any time after chapter 3) or at the end of the course. If you introduce the project early, you can set aside class periods (or half-periods) throughout the course to work on the different steps outlined below. If you introduce the project at the end, you can give students several consecutive days to complete the work.

If it is appropriate for your class, give students the option to work in pairs.

Step #1: Choose a Subject

Timing: Half a class period

Students should complete the chart on page 71 in the student journal. They now decide on a subject. They may choose a person mentioned in their journal, such as a biblical character or someone in Jewish history from one of the Values in Action exercises. If it is appropriate for your class, give students the option to research someone from the Bible or Jewish history that they have not learned about in the course and who demonstrates one or more of the values they studied. Students need to receive teacher approval for a person not mentioned in the course and explain which values that person demonstrates.

If you introduce the project early in the course, students will need to choose a person from the material they have already studied. If you introduce the project at the end of the course, they will be able to choose a person from any chapter in the course.

Step #2: Learn about Your Subject

Timing: Two classes, or one class and work at home

Students individually complete the questions on page 71 of their journals. Then, in pairs, they review their charts to receive feedback from a classmate, such as suggestions for research questions and how/where to find the answers.

If your school or synagogue has a library, take your students there and explain how to find relevant materials. Make sure to have as many computers as possible available for student use.

Step #3: Prepare Your Presentation

Timing: Two classes, or one class and work at home

Students independently answer the questions on page 72 of their journals and then review their answers in pairs to receive feedback.

Make sure to have as many computers as possible available for student use. Also make sure that students have any other materials or tools they need for their projects, such as poster board or a phone to take videos.

Step #4: Present Your Project

Timing: One evening or class period, and time for reflection at the beginning of the next time you meet

If possible, host a special event at your school and invite the students' families and/or other classes in the school to attend. At the event, students present their projects. If a special evening is not possible, students present their projects in class.

In the class following the students' presentations, they should receive your feedback and reflect on their projects by responding to the prompts on page 72 in the student journal. In pairs, students share something that they learned from working on the project.

Glossary

Acharayut — responsibility

Aliyah — immigration (literally: going up) to Israel

Bitachon — trust

B'tzelem Elohim — in the image of God

Chesed — kindness

Emet — truth

Kinah — jealousy

Lech lecha — "Go forth" (from the story of Abram and Sarai)

Midah — character trait

Midrash — rabbinic interpretation of biblical text

Ometz leiv — strength of heart, courage

Sh'lom bayit — peace in the home

Tzaddik — righteous person

Tzedakah — charity or righteousness

Notes